D1624258

For.
Marsha Kress Lonergan,

from one coal cracker to another

Best Wishes,

Francis Norton Gallagher

4/13/85

The Only Western Town in the East
Part II

Short Stories by
F. N. Gallagher

J.R. & G. CO 4165 GREENWOOD DRIVE. • *Bethlehem, Pa* 18017

All the characters herein portrayed are fictitious, and any resemblance to actual persons, living or dead, is purely coincidental.

Copyright © 1982 by F. N. Gallagher

All rights reserved

ISBN 0-9608844-0-8

Printed in the United States of America

For my oldest friend John A. Rogers of Harrisburg, Pa. who might have told these stories better than I have.

Contents

Foreword

Dear Reader,

WHEN WE WERE LAST in touch, I was engaged in conversation with Joe Topton, the news scribe from the *Shenandoah Herald,* the only newspaper in the only western town in the east, who imparted to me the pleasant information that Gus Lynn, the left handed pugilist had, through the combined efforts of Handsome Earley, the Irish Undertaker and Len Sak, the Polish mortician, secured the job of grave digger in the Shenandoah Catholic cemetery. This good fortune resulted from Gus's keen perception of Len Sak slipping a "mickey" into the double vodka on the rocks which was later imbibed by "The Ace" which caused him to sleep more soundly, even though he was an unwilling victim of narcolepsy, a disease known to ordinary people like myself as severe sleeping sickness. The fear of the revelation of this fact to Large George, the barroom impressario, by Gus Lynn, was the catalyst for the action taken by the conniving but somewhat perturbed entrepreneurs.

In *The Only Western Town In the East—Part One,* I described a series of certain incidents and the behavior of certain individuals which were peculiar to the area of the coal regions of northeastern Pennsylvania during the period of the Great Depression and Prohibition. All of the activities described had actually taken place, with some embellishments on my part.

Response from the first volume was very gratifying but I detected, primarily from people not affiliated with the region, the conception that all the residents and all the activities were comical in nature. This was not the case. A far greater percentage of the residents was made up of normal, middle class Americans whose lives and activities did not lend themselves to a humorous story teller like myself. No doubt there were incidents which might have intrigued authors such as Bellaman, Saroyan, or Faulkner. That this area of the United States had its share of skeletons in the closet was proven many years ago, most admirably, by my illustrious distant cousin, John O'Hara.

In this volume, while continuing in a humorous style in the first four tales, I veer from the role of quipster and wag to sage in telling of the lives of Bobby Glendower and my Uncle Christopher. I hope you like it.

The Author.

"Mrs. America"

THE CATALYST FOR THE entire episode that I am about to relate is my watching television. Normally I watch television as often as I brush my teeth, which is when I get up in the morning and when I go to bed at night. On each occasion as I check the tube, I am forced to observe which country is starting a new war, who is running for office, who is being murdered or what crook is writing his latest book and other gems of knowledge that are thrust at me as I patiently await the sports report, which is all I am interested in anyway.

For I am in the gambling profession, known as someone who will take a bet on anything, even a prize fight, and who always maintained his reputation of never having welched on a bet. I learned the intricasies of my profession at the feet of Honest Pete, the renowned Philly gambler, who before he passed away from cancer became famous in 1948 when he made a fortune backing Harry S. Truman over Thomas E. Dewey. While it was known mostly among the gambling fraternity, back in 1936 he made book against the German dirigible Hindenburg, betting that it would come to its fatal demise before the end of 1937. He was proven right, when in May of that year, the air ship burst into flames and crashed in Lakewood, N.J.

When Honest Pete became aware that he would shortly be transported to meet the great gambler in the sky, he became even more famous when he offered to the general public, a price of ten to one, against the choice of which of the seven days of the week he would take his final journey, with all the profit from the caper being donated to the Damon Runyon cancer fund, so it is easy to see how I acquired my skill.

As I was awaiting the sports report on the tube, I was amazed to see a picture of a former girl friend of mine receiving a check for $5000.00, for winning the title of Mrs. America. This was not a big event, as is the Miss America contest held annually in Atlantic City, N.J., but it must have been very important to a young lady from Hazleton, Pa., whose maiden name was Sally Flaherty and whose name now is Mrs. Phillip Sherman of Stamford, Conn., which came as no great surprise to me.

As I took in all the details of the presentation, my thoughts went back, like a film in fast reverse, to a warm summer in the 1930's, when I was young and foolish.

It took me back to the time of the great Depression and the beginning of the enormous initial binge. To start with, there was the N.R.A. for the National Recovery Act, the W.P.A. for the Works Progress Administration, the T.V.A. for the Tennessee Valley Authority, the P.W.A. for the Public Works Administration, and the C.C.C. for the Civilian Conservation Corps, not to mention the F.P.C. for the Federal Power Commission and many, many more. It was said at the time that every letter of the alphabet found its way into the abbreviation of some government project, and some even said that had it not been for the W.P.A., most people would have become communists.

The C.C.C. was unique in that it took all the growing sons of the poor and unemployed, fed them well, employed them in various endeavors, not the least of which was to train them in regimentation and obedience, and in the overall, prepare them for the war which was soon to follow. This at least suggested that all the high noses in Washington, D.C. were not necessarily lame brains, as was the general consensus.

But with all the initialed programs, there was not one which could aid or succor the growing daughters. As for them, some people said in jest, though I sometimes wonder, that all female children over and above the number required to do the house work, should be sent to China and have their feet bound, as was the practice in that enlightened country and the net result would be less mouths to feed. Other suggestions, slightly more believable, hinted that all excess daughters be placed in various nunneries across the land, but this was impractical as all the convents and missions were already overcrowded with daughters who, needing bread and board, had already thought of the idea long before my deep thinking contemporaries.

So you can see that this was a tough time to live and the growing daughters had it just as severe as the growing sons, particularly if you were poor, which meant nearly everyone in the Anthracite region of Eastern Pennsylvania.

Sally Flaherty was an exception to the rule. She was not poor, her father was important in Luzerne County politics, she was a clerk and typist in the county office of the W.P.A. and in addition to all that, she owned a car, a red 1936 Chevrolet convertible, no less. She had red hair, an engaging smile with beautiful teeth, a figure like Betty Grable, and a job. Even more, she was single and had much more going for her than the average growing daughter of the time.

The first time I saw her was at a Thursday night dance at Lakewood Park near Mahanoy City, during the time of the Big Bands. Lakewood Park featured the best. Each Thursday night there was a different band. Among others were Paul Whiteman, both Jimmy and Tommy Dorsey, Mal Hallet, Harry James, Ted Weems, and Gene Goldkette. James' band featured a skinny vocalist named Frank Sinatra and Ted Weems answered with another Italian American, Perry Como.

Not all the thousands in the audience were dancers. Hundreds crowded about the bandstand and just listened to the marvelous music; I was one of those. During intermissions, people retreated to one of the four bars, where 3.2 beer was sold, Prohibition having been recently repealed. The demand for beer at the tap became so great and it flowed so rapidly,

3

that it was almost impossible to keep the beer cold with normal cooling equipment. One man was kept busy just tapping beer kegs, which emptied in record time.

As I was standing in the crowd listening to Ted Weems play the recent Rogers and Hart tune, *Mountain Greenery,* which was being whistled by that incomparable whistler, Elmo Tanner, Sally Flaherty stepped on my shoe, which started the whole affair.

After the usual apology on her part, and the think nothing of it on mine, I asked if I might buy her a beer and to my amazement, she said yes.

As we drank our beer and made the usual small talk about the band and the qualities of Perry Como's voice, she said she had to leave and meet a girl friend in front of the bandstand, but before she did, I asked if I might see her again, to which she replied, "Why not. How about next Thursday night in front of the bandstand?"

So I saw her the following Thursday night and the one after that and I finally acquired the courage and asked if she would go out with me some evening. Her response was rather odd, saying Monday, Tuesday, or Thursday evenings were fine, but that she was unavailable the other nights of the week.

I should have gotten the message at once but I didn't. It should have been quite apparent that she had a steady engagement every other night of the week, which in that era, were called date nights.

We saw quite a bit of each other that summer and on each occasion she would insist that we drive to remote parts of eastern Pennsylvania in my 1931 Model A Ford and occasionally in her handsome convertible coupe.

We never frequented bars or night clubs in or near Hazleton or Shenandoah, where there were an abundance of night spots and we always wound up in strange, far away places. One of her favorite spots was Lake Nuangola, near Wilkes Barre, where we would rent a row boat and watch the moon rise over the eastern rim of the lake. It was a beautiful setting, but I had the feeling that she seemed to feel safer the further we got from shore.

One night in a bar in Mount Carmel, Pa., she suddenly said that we had to leave at once and we all but ran out of the place. Suddenly the pieces of the puzzle began to fall into place. It finally occured to me that she was afraid of being watched or followed, which accounted for her enthusiasm to frequent out of the way places. Furthermore, it explained her peculiar habit of carefully looking up and down the street each time she got out of an automobile.

The final piece of the puzzle fell into place the following week. As I was crossing the intersection of Main and Center streets in Shenandoah, a long Cadillac stopped at the traffic light and I saw Sally Flaherty sitting in the passenger's side of the front seat. Driving the car was a man I recognized as Phil Sherman, the number one man in the slot machine and pin ball business in Schuylkill County. When I waved to Sally as I passed the front of the car, she totally ignored me, trying to give the impression that I had confused her with someone else. When she abruptly looked away as I crossed the street, it became clear to me that she didn't want Sherman to think that she knew me at all.

The next time I saw Sally, I pressed her for the reason for all the subterfuge and she confessed that she was Sherman's steady girl on date nights and she was afraid of what he might do if he became aware that she was seeing someone else.

When I told her I could handle Sherman with weights on both my legs and with one arm tied behind my back, she did not seem to be impressed and suggested that we stop seeing each other. This made me all the more persistent, for in my youthful folly, it never occured to me that his anger might be directed at her and not at me.

So she relented and I continued to see her as the summer faded into fall.

Later on, I was to pick her up at her home and my Model A Ford developed trouble and I could not get it started. When

5

I called her to relate my problem, she offered to pick me up in the convertible and take me to her home in Hazleton, which she did and where she spent most of the evening trying to terminate the romance, even though I could easily tell that she truly felt otherwise.

About 11:00 PM, her father came in and when he became aware that I had no transportation, he suggested that I return to Shenandoah on the bus, the last of which was to leave Hazleton at 1:00 AM, saying that he did not want Betty to drive back to Hazleton alone at that time of night.

As you might have guessed, due to my classic stupidity, I continued my conversation with Sally too long, and it was with a lonesome feeling that I watched the last bus pull away, beyond the reach of my desperate attempts to hail it.

However, luck was with me. As I stood at the southern edge of Hazleton trying to hitch a ride, I was picked up by the very first car, which took me as far as Brandonville. I was but about two miles from Shenandoah and I began walking home.

At a remote part of the road, near the crest of the Brandonville Hill, a black Cadillac stopped to pick me up and who was driving the car but Phil Sherman.

At the time he was tall and extremely thin. He was good-looking in a southern European sort of way with coal black hair, piercing eyes, sharp features and an aquiline nose. He would at first look give the impression that he was of Italian heritage, but in as much as I was familiar with his family, I knew him to be Jewish and from a very Orthodox family as well.

It always had been my understanding that young Jewish men confined their attentions to young Jewish girls, this being the rule rather than the exception, so I was always puzzled by his attraction to Sally, and even more so by her attraction to him, with her being of Irish Catholic descent.

While Sherman was reputed to be a shady character, he nevertheless maintained a normal profile of life style, for being in the slot machine business was looked on lightly as compared to other underworld operations, such as the rampant prostitution prevalent in the region at the time.

I was not seated in the front seat of the Cadillac but ten seconds when my arms were pinned to the seat by a man who had been hiding in the back seat. I could barely move my shoulders as the man in the back seemed abnormally strong and I began thrashing violently with my feet and legs.

My powerful resisting came to a sudden stop as Sherman removed a pistol from an inside pocket, placed the end of the barrel against my ear and said, "Sit still."

I became as meek as a lamb immediately. Never before or since have I known such fright, as I realized that if he pulled the trigger, my brain would be splashed all over the interior of the car. I hardly breathed. I pleaded with him to remove the gun, promising I would keep still and offer no resistance. Slowly he pulled the gun away and I breathed a sigh of relief, even though the man in the rear of the car still held my arms.

Sherman then passed the pistol back to the man in the rear seat, who told me to keep looking straight ahead, which I did at once. I had no way of knowing if he had the gun pointed at me or not.

Sherman began talking. He told me that what was happening now was but to frighten me, as he had no intention of harming me at this time. However, he also said that I must forget Sally Flaherty, never see her again, nor even call her by phone. This I promised on my life, after which he drove to Shenandoah, where I got out of the car and felt that the weight of the world had been removed from my shoulders.

I stopped going to the Thursday dances at Lakewood Park, I never went to Hazleton again, and I never learned who was in the back seat on that fateful night.

Several weeks later, I read in the Shenandoah Herald that Miss Sally Flaherty, daughter of Mr. & Mrs. Thomas Flaherty of Hazleton had become the wife of Mr. Phillip Sherman of Shenandoah and would shortly take up residence in Stamford, Conn.

In a way I was both sorry and glad to read this, as I would miss our little get togethers but I was glad that she had moved from Hazleton, which would make it all the more likely that I would never see her again, which actually came to pass, for the very next time I saw her was tonite, on T.V., when she won the Mrs. America contest.

As I sat in front of the T.V. set and the late, late movie droned on and on and as I finished my reverie, I contemplated two things. First I wondered if Sherman had used any undue influence on the judges of the contest and second, if my dear friend Honest Pete were still alive, and knew the situation as I did, what kind of odds would he have lain that Sally Flaherty Sherman would become Mrs. America.

"The 1931 Dodge Coupe"

ON A LATE AUTUMN AFTERNOON during Prohibition, I am
riding the streets of Shenandoah, Pa. in the passenger seat of
a 1931 Dodge coupe, to the front grille of which is attached
a mounted tire on a wheel, which gives the vehicle more than
a rather odd appearance. At the controls of the car is one
Ignotz Hemmelweis, the eldest son of the Jewish family of the
same name that resides on Oak St.

How a family acquires a monicker like Hemmelweis is in
itself beyond comprehension, but to preface it with the first
name of Ignotz is too cruel to contemplate. Ignotz, who is
called Iggie for short, suffers much embarrasment and ridicule
because of his peculiar handle and I find a soft spot in my heart
for him, as he is a pitiful character to begin with, even without
his outlandish name.

He is short, rather pudgy, has crooked teeth and wears
glasses, the lenses of which are coke bottle thick. He has a
slight limp, and on top of it all just got out of jail.

It seems that Iggie's papa, Old Sam Hemmelweis, is in the
bootlegging business, having been successful in that profession for the past ten years. Two years ago when Iggie becomes
twenty-one, or legal age, Old Sam transfers the ownership of
the whiskey business to his fine son Iggie, who is now of
sufficient age to reap the benefits of the business, which to
Iggie is but a measly salary, what with Old Sam keeping the
lion's share of the handsome profit. Not only does Iggie reap
just a measly salary, but he also assumes all the risks, the
business now being in his name.

9

And so it comes to pass that two years ago, the Federal Revenue Agents apprehend Iggie in the process of delivering a load of homemade booze to a customer on South Main Street, in Shenandoah and the upshot of the whole miserable debacle is simply that Iggie goes to college for two one year semesters in the Eastern Penitentiary in Philadelphia.

However, Iggie is not only an ex-con, but is also a bear for punishment, for at this very moment, in the rear baggage trunk of the Dodge coupe, are ten five gallon cans of homemade whiskey. He is quite aware that should he be apprehended again by the Revenue people, he would be required to return to the Philly jail where his term might be extended sufficiently for him to acquire a degree in prison behavior and decorum. Even so, he does not seem to be impeded in his unwavering determination to deliver the contraband liquor to a speakeasy on West Center Street.

The bad judgement displayed by Iggie in this escapade is exceeded only by my own stupidity, for should the Revenuers catch Iggie while I am in his company in the Dodge coupe, not only Iggie, but yours truly might spend a few years in the Philly jail at government expense. But in as much as Iggie is a good customer of mine in my numbers writing profession, and my own inherent curiosity getting the better of me, I take the chance and accompany Iggie to the West Center Street speakeasy.

Iggie's Dodge coupe requires a description. The door handle and lock to the rear trunk space are smashed, probably by a heavy hammer, and the latch is in the "locked" position, giving the justifiable impression that access to the compartment is impossible. This is half true, in as much as the door to the trunk cannot be opened, but Iggie has ingeniously arranged the interior of the passenger section so that by pulling a lever, the right seat automatically moves forward, allowing easy entry to the trunk space, as the partition between the rear of the right seat and the rear trunk compartment has been previously removed.

The rear springs are oversized, and when the trunk space is empty, the automobile rides abnormally high in the rear, but when carrying ten five gallon cans of his product, the vehicle rides normally, giving no impression of overload.

When I remark to Iggie that his subterfuge is unique, he informs me that it has saved him on several occasions, but on one occurrence an inquisitive agent asks him what he does for a spare wheel and tire, which leaves Iggie temporarily nonplussed, but he escapes by promising the law man that he will at once purchase a wheel and tire and tie it securely to the front grille of the Dodge coupe. This Iggie accomplishes without buying anything, for at his first secluded opportunity, he removes the spare wheel and tire from the trunk and securely adheres it to the front grille as he has promised. Ergo, the peculiar appearance of the Dodge coupe.

So as we proceed west on Center Street, the Dodge coupe seems to be as normal in appearance as any other vehicle, with the exception of the odd location of the spare wheel and tire, not withstanding the fact that ten five gallon cans of homemade whiskey, worth thirty dollars a can, are safely ensconced in the trunk of the car.

The making of the whiskey is a story in itself. Each five gallon can consists of two and one-half gallons of alcohol and two and one-half gallons of tap water, with a spot of vanilla extract to supply color and taste. It is Iggie's handiwork, mixed by himself in his father's drop or hideout in an obscure garage in a back alley in the southern part of the town.

Every week, a truck owned by Jake the Fake, the numbers and booze boss of South Philly, delivers several hundred five gallon cans of the alcohol to the drop, where Iggie has to do the unloading. The driver is then paid in spot cash at the rate of ten dollars per can. One need not be an Einstein to compute the enormous profit for Old Sam.

When we arrive at the speakeasy rear door, which opens on an alley, Iggie opens the secret entry to the trunk, carries the ten cans into the back room of the establishment, collects his three hundred dollars, and as we drive away, I breathe a sigh of relief for though I have done some foolish things in my non-violent career, like being a willing witness to the waking of the Ace in Handsome Early's funeral emporium, this caper surely tops them all.

At my request, Iggie drops me off at John the Greek's restaurant on Main St. where I calm my nerves with a cup of Joe and a strawberry tart.

The next time I connect with Iggie is in the dead of winter and it happens as I am leaving Large George's saloon on Coal St., and the snow is about a foot deep. As I am about to cross the street, Iggie pulls up in the Dodge coupe and I can tell from the elevated rear section of the vehicle that Iggie is not delivering any booze, so I accept the ride he graciously offers.

One look at Iggy tells me that all is not well with him, as he has a bandage on his forehead, the area around his left eye is black and blue and his right cheek is swollen to grapefruit size, and his demeanor is lower than the Titanic. Naturally I inquire about how all this damage and somberness comes to pass and Iggie's reply is sad indeed.

"Last week", says Iggie, "I have it out with Old Sam, saying that I am no longer going to be his lackey and that I want at least one half of the profit from the business, which I consider a fair offer, but Old Sam becomes unexpectedly violent. While I am attempting to calm him down and am totally unprepared, Sam removes his blackjack, which he always carries in his right rear pocket and strikes me on the forehead, rendering me unconscious. While I am in dream land, he goes to work on me, the results of which are easily seen. When I awaken, Sam tells me that this is only a sample and should I repeat my indiscretion he will give me the whole treatment, all the while lecturing me that my behaviour is not representative of the son of a Jewish father."

"So you see," says Iggie, "I am lower than ten below and do not know what to do."

This is truly a sad state of affairs and I feel for Iggie with my heart, for I've known him most of my life. We graduated together from J. W. Cooper High School some years back, and all through the school years he is subjected to racial slurs as well as constant ridicule by most of his peers due to his Shylockian appearance, and his atrocious name.

I immediately try to console Iggie, telling him that things cannot become worse and that as long as I am around he will have at least one friend. But trying to uplift Iggie is as hard as raising the dead, for even when I tell him that I will accompany him on his next delivery, and even help him carry the cans, he shows no visible effect of my Galahadian offer.

Suddenly I think of a story my mother tells me the day my father passes away when I am but twelve years old, which I immediately relate to Iggie, and it goes as follows.

A great Chinese Emperor living in the distant past, on pain of death ordered his court seer to prepare one sentence which would encompass all the joys and all the sorrows known in the world. After considerable thought, the seer replied as follows, "YOUR MAJESTY, AND THIS TOO SHALL PASS."

When I relate the story to Iggie, he seems a bit more hopeful and when he drops me off at my place, I say goodbye, but cannot get Iggie out of my mind.

It is but two weeks later that I am the sole witness to the heist of Mike Carey's bar on South Main St. when Rocco Sartori banishes me from Shenandoah for the rest of my life, and even though my banishment lasts but a short time due to Rocco's sudden incarceration, other problems develop and slowly but surely I forget about poor Iggie.

However, during my banishment, I make Lew Tendler's booze joint on South Broad St. in Philly my temporary business headquarters and it is there that I am contacted by Soldier Jim, the R. A. F. aerial gunner, who among other things tells me that Iggie has flown the roost, taking off in the 1931 Dodge coupe and has not been heard of since.

As time goes by, I get to think less and less of Iggie but

when I do, and feel sorry for him, I console myself by remembering the story of the Chinese Emperor.

During the years that follow, I become involved in many peculiar events, but always maintain my reputation as a nonviolent person except during the years of World War No. Two, during which time I follow in the footsteps of Soldier Jim and become an aerial gunner in the Army Air Corps, but that is another story.

One thing that I can be justly accused of is being a romantic, especially when I am possessed of the grape, and am a sucker for nostalgia and the good old days, and so, when it comes to pass, I appear at the twenty-fifth annual reunion of my high school class and who is there, larger than life, but my friend Iggie.

When we get together there is much hand shaking and embracing for I am truly glad to see Iggie, even though some of our contemporaries seem less inclined to be so demonstrative.

Iggie's appearance requires some telling. He is decked out in a shark skin suit of a somber gray color, a black Homburg hat, gray spats, and carries a gold headed cane to aid him with his long afflicting limp. He is the picture of success, having arrived at the affair in a chauffeur-driven limousine and is spending money as if it were going out of style.

When I inquire of Iggie of how all this came to pass, he tells me so.

"I learn of your banishment," says Iggie, "from Mrs. Betty F., the local rich widow who is one of the few people who will talk to me at the time of my trouble, and I am much taken back by your misfortune when I come to the realization that I have lost my best friend. However, Mrs. Betty F. is kind to me in my innocence and I learn much from her, such as stock market tips and the like, but the most important thing she makes me aware of is the manner in which I can remove myself from the tentacles of Old Sam which I do as follows."

14

"The first thing I do is rent my own drop, which is located in a garage but a half block from Old Sam's. Each week, when the shipment arrives, I remove one-third of the alcohol from each can, transferring the stuff to empty ones which I cache in my own hideout. I then refill Old Sam's cans with tap water, and the only people who might become aware of the difference in the booze are the people who drink the stuff, and I consider that what I am doing is a favor to them, as half and half mixture is close to a lethal dose. However, no one even suspects that the booze is diluted, as drinkers in Shenandoah will drink anything, as long as it provides the desired effect."

"Within a year I have almost filled my garage with the cans of alcohol and I am ready to branch out on my own. I weaken the recipe of the concoction even more than I do with Old Sam's stuff, and I find some new customers. I sell part of my supply to Old Sam's accounts, but he hardly notices the loss in revenue and I continue merrily on my way toward financial independence, all the while taking care of the 1931 Dodge coupe as I proceed."

"I keep all my cash in a metal fire proof World War One ammunition box in the trunk of the Dodge coupe, as I do not trust banks, knowing very well that knowledge of any noticeable increase in my account would in all likelihood leak back to Old Sam, through the chicanery of unscrupulous bank directors."

"I set my goal at ten G's, which I accumulate in less than a year after I begin selling the stuff and when the last can is sold, I make my move."

"On a bright summer morning, during the time of your banishment, with all my earthly possessions stashed in the Dodge coupe, most important of which being the ten big ones safely hidden in the trunk, I say goodbye to Shenandoah, and following the advice of Mr. Greeley, go west, without even a note or a farewell to Old Sam."

"I have no fear of being apprehended for auto theft, or any

other charge for that matter, as Old Sam is totally aware that if I am arrested I will immediately turn state's evidence and tell my story to the Feds, to see to it that Old Sam accompanies me on the mandatory trip to the Philly jail. I figure my past experience in the slammer will benefit me greatly and furthermore Old Sam does not have many summers left and will enjoy his forced vacation far less than I."

"I take a leisurely and delightful cross country trip and I am astonished at the beauty of this benevolent land, and considering what is going on at the time in Germany, I am overjoyed that I am alive in America in the 1930's, even though I am Jewish and less than good looking."

"When I arrive in Los Angeles five weeks later, the first thing I do is legally change my name. I am now known as Craig Reynolds, which has a WASPish sound, and is infinitely better than Ignotz Hemmelweis. Two weeks after I arrive, and after careful consideration and investigating, I make a substantial down payment toward the purchase of an automobile junk yard business, using most of my ten G's, which in those days is a lot of moola."

"Over the years," says Iggie, "due to my natural ability to rearrange cars, as proven by what I do to my Dodge coupe, my business grows in leaps and bounds, so I branch out with several junk yards in the L.A. area, and I end up with many people on my payroll."

"The junk yard business in California is a sure thing, for as you are aware, the citizens out there wear out their cars faster than they wear out their shoes, and there is always a good supply of old and new junkers that I buy and turn into ready cash by selling replacement parts."

"One thing more," says Iggie, "at my largest junk yard in south Los Angeles, I erect a huge platform, at least forty feet high, where, still with the spare wheel and tire securely attached to the front grille, rests the 1931 Dodge coupe, on the sides of which are emblazoned the words "Reynolds Auto

Parts—Cash Only," which always reminds me of my humble beginnings."

The very last thing that Iggie says to me as he leaves is as follows:

"I'LL SEE YOU AT OUR FIFTIETH REUNION."

A Case of Mistaken Identity

IT IS A WARM THURSDAY night in a summer of the late 1930s and I am standing in front of the band stand at Lakewood Park in Barnesville, Pa. listening to Paul Whiteman's orchestra play George Gershwin's *Rhapsody In Blue*. The music is so inspiring that the thousand or more couples dancing in the huge edifice come to a gradual stop and for the following five or more minutes, it is not a dance joint but a concert hall. As the dancing ceases, the sound of sliding shoes over the polished floor comes to a slow halt and by its absence, the music becomes all the more beautiful.

The Thursday Night Dances, as they are called at the time, provide a weekly get together of people from all over the anthracite coal region of northeastern Pennsylvania.

Among the dancers in attendance are Ruth Mast, the Shenandoah beauty whose stellar performances in "The Bat," "China Doll," and "Smiling Through" for the Schuylkill County Theater Guild have prompted Warner Brothers to ask her to take a film test. Ruth is escorted by Johnny Schmidt, the Shenandoah brewery heir, who might be the only Shenandoah native rich enough to provide Ruth with all her necessities. Also from Shenandoah are Peggy and Handsome Early, the funeral people, who achieve Schuylkill County immortality by waking "The Ace" in their funeral home, long before his actual demise. Harry and Grace Tierney are there. They own the dance hall and most everything else in Mahanoy City, Pa. Also from Mahanoy City is Joe Kiley, the local postmaster, who is six feet, six inches tall and dances with his wife Helen,

18

who is about four feet, eleven inches and has to shout to be heard.

Pottsville is represented by Bill Mainwaring, the accomplished first baseman of the Pine Grove Athletics, who is potentially another Lou Gehrig but won't leave Schuylkill County. He dances with Dottie Wasley, recently divorced from her husband "Rip," who is big in Schuylkill County road construction, both of whom never get over being referred to in John O'Hara's *Appointment in Samarra*. Also from Pottsville is Les Hemmerly, the physical culture nut, who gains a county wide reputation when, after downing two straight vodkas, he amazes the customers in Joe Rice's gin mill in Frackville by walking the entire length of the bar on his hands and never disturbs one glass or ashtray. Les is dancing with Amanda Dawson, the utility executive's daughter, who is built like Betty Grable and for whom I have a secret desire, even though I have the reputation of steering clear of dames. Personally I feel that all dames spell trouble, but Amanda is such a sweet pea that maybe the trouble would be worth it, but I do not approach her remembering my unfortunate experience with Sally Flaherty of Hazleton, when I nearly have my head blown off by Phil Sherman of Shenandoah for doing little more than looking twice at beautiful Sally, but that is another story. From Hazleton comes Harry Paul, the sports scribe, who writes only about the New York Yankees, giving the impression that all other major league teams belong in Tibet, as his readers never find out anything about them except the team which is unfortunate enough to have been defeated by the Yanks. Harry is dancing with Jennie Bimot, the Hazleton socialite who is a sure bet to become a member of Dr. Bob and Bill Wilson's A.A. group in Akron, Ohio. Lansford is represented by Jim McHall, the political authority who is being investigated by the Feds for tax evasion and is accompanied by Mary Gaughan, daughter of the Coaldale surgeon, who is an up and coming socialite and who lives only for an invitation to the Pottsville Assembly next New Year's Eve, which will, she thinks, guarantee her position in northeastern Pennsylvania society forever. From no one knows where, comes a beautiful brunette called Rosita, who will not divulge her last name and is the spitting image of Hedy Lamarr, lovely beyond description in a tight fitting but socially acceptable dress, spike heels, magnificent legs, teeth like pearls and a soft southern drawl. She dances with, and only with, Mike Murphy, the Shenandoah automobile dealer who is single and has the reputation of squiring beautiful women.

Rosita and Mike attend the last four Thursday night dances together and although one and all dances with any sweet pea he cares to ask, no one but Mike as much as lays a hand on Rosita.

Why Mike Murphy will hardly allow Rosita to talk with anyone, let alone dance with the afore mentioned males, all of whom most certainly have asked her, is beyond my comprehension, for most people who attend these affairs are not necessarily loving couples but dance adherents who enjoy variety and who are not necessarily trying to making a conquest. But Mike is most insistent, as well as big and tough, and would not hesitate to belt one in the kisser should he be so inclined. So one and all leave Rosita to Mike but there is much conversation about Rosita, with the women folk commenting that she is a very good looking dame and not without good manners, and all the men stating that they had somehow seen her before, but when it had taken place, she had been a blonde.

There are many more noteworthy personalities at the dance, some from as far north as Scranton and several from Philadelphia, but it would take much too long to enumerate them and describe their noteworthiness.

The characters that I make previous reference to all have one more thing in common. They are all friends of Sammy Cole, the proprieter of the exclusive booze joint in Park Crest, Pa. This Sammy Cole is a gray haired aristocratic character of about fifty summers. He becomes very well known after

World War I as he is at one time a pilot in the Lafayette Escadrille, has four German planes to his credit, and is a close friend of Eddie Rickenbacker. He runs his exclusive gin mill at the same location since 1920 and though at that time he dispenses bootleg booze, his joint seemed to be off limits to the law enforcement agencies, as he was never disturbed by the revenue agents and he would give one the impression that the eighteenth amendment to the Constitution had never been enacted.

Sammy does not advertize, needless to say did not do so during Prohibition, and sees no reason for doing so now, even though the Volstead Act is now repealed.

Not everyone can get into Sammy's joint. One gains entry only by a reference from an approved customer and the sponsor is held responsible for the behaviour of his protegé. Sammy is familiar with the lineage of most all his customers, having served their parents in the distant past and the joint is almost as exclusive as the Union League in Philly or at least the Pottsville Club, but not nearly as impressive.

Sammy's joint gives the impression of a large bungalow, separated from its neighbors by at least an acre of ground, and all its windows are blacked out with heavy curtains. Except for the abnormally high number of parked automobiles, one would get the impression that there was no one inside.

I, myself, am a friend of Sammy's and have entry to his fine establishment due to my steering him to a sure thing, and how this takes place requires some telling.

It seems that back in 1936, the Shenandoah Presidents professional football team is to play the Reading Keys in an important match. On the Friday preceeding the game, I am sitting in John the Greek's restaurant in Shenandoah having a cup of Joe and who comes in but Sammy, and I buy him a coffee. Sammy knows who I am by his relationship with my father who before his demise, is big in Schuylkill County medicine and is a regular customer at Sammy's joint. Suddenly I am called to the phone and the caller is my friend, Honest

Pete, the Philly gambler, who provides me with an astonishing piece of news. He says that word gets to him that Benny Nork Jr., the all-America fullback at the University of Pennsylvania will play for the Presidents on the coming Sunday, using an assumed name, and will receive two hundred one spots from Joe Pauley, the President's owner, for his services. This is quite a bit of news as I am aware that should Benny Jr. be apprehended he will lose his amateur status as well as his expected job of backfield coach at Harvard next year, the fruits of which are to pay his tuition and board as he pursues his law degree. I do not ask Pete how he comes to know all this for by answering Pete would violate the professional gamblers' code, but I do know that with Benny Nork Jr. playing for the Presidents, they are a sure thing, as Benny is the best football player this side of Jim Thorpe.

When I return to the table, Sammy has been joined by Mike Murphy, who is the previously mentioned escort of the beautiful Rosita and as they are my friends, I swear them to secrecy and impart to them the knowledge made available to me by Honest Pete.

As anyone interested in Pennsylvania sports will know, the Presidents defeat the Keys, 20 to 7, with a new phenomenon named Matt Rice, who is no one but Benny Nork Jr., scoring two touchdowns and kicking two field goals and Sammy Cole, Mike Murphy, and yours truly make a killing on the scam. To return to the dance.

All the dames previously mentioned have another common interest. They are members of the Schuylkill County Ladies Auxiliary, an organization that meets each Tuesday afternoon in the Necho Allen Hotel in Pottsville. After a lunch and more than a few cocktails, one and all visit the county jail to give support and advice to women who are down on their luck and who have been confined for various reasons from child abuse to drunkenness to prostitution, some of which are unlucky enough to be arrested in raids on bordellos, such as the Stucco in Shenandoah, Big Mary's in Park Crest, and The Red Door on Railroad Street in Pottsville. The auxiliary is reputed to be a fine organization and it is well known that on many occasions they return erring females from a life of sin to respectability as it is known in the late 1930's in northeastern Pennsylvania. It is also well known that though the organization has some success, the underlying reason for the Tuesday afternoon meetings is simply another opportunity to belt the grog.

When Paul Whiteman and his orchestra play Auld Lang Syne, with the vocal by Jane Froman, all hands prepare to leave and as it is only 12:30 A.M., the shank of the evening in Schuylkill County, I immediately leave for Sammy's joint to join in the usual post-dance soirée.

As I enter, I become aware of Frank Bellet, the Schuylkill County bank giant, standing at the bar. Frank is a member of the board of directors in nine area banks and is always loaded with cash as well as booze. Sitting alone in the corner of the room, appearing as inconspicuous as possible, is Frank's chauffer and body guard, a guy called Big Jack, who has the reputation of being the toughest goon in eastern Pennsylvania, which is a large admonition.

Frank is known far and wide for his peculiar and expensive habit of disliking to touch silver. Whenever he buys anything, even the ten cent glass of beer that he buys for me when I enter, he leaves all the silver for the bartender. He never has silver in his pockets but is always equipped with a huge roll of bills, the denominations of which being known to none but Frank himself. No one ever tries to roll Frank for they would have Big Jack to contend with and it is rumored that Big Jack even sleeps in the same room with Frank in his large home in Shenandoah.

I take a seat at the bar directly across the room from the lovely Amanda Dawson, who is my secret yen, in order to look at her as much as possible, which is very easy on the eyes. But I still leave an opening to observe the behaviour of Sammy's other guests, as is my wont.

If I have a weakness, it is my curiosity in the nature of

human behaviour. Just sitting and watching and listening to characters such as these is my therapy.

As I look across the room I observe the beautiful Rosita and her escort Mike Murphy sitting at the same table as Handsome and Peggy Early. This seems to me to be a peculiar combination as Peggy Early is looked upon as the grand dame of Schuylkill County society and is known to fraternize with only well known W.A.S.P.S. or genteel, lace curtain Irish. It is well known around and about that Mike Murphy's real name is Murkowski and was changed legally to Murphy by his father, an immigrant coal miner. So to see Peggy and Mike Murphy together is rather odd when one recalls that Peggy has snubbed Mike many times in the past, not the least of which is her failure to invite him to the many cocktail parties she throws in her home in Shenandoah.

There is much good cheer in the group, but one and all are stunned by the beautiful Rosita. Mike escorts her to all the remaining tables in the joint, introducing her simply as Rosita, as though she has no last name.

Rosita is so demure and well mannered that most of the female characters in the place do not seem to resent her, as most female characters do with beautiful dames, and there are many occasions to observe Rosita and other women in the group retreat to the ladies room to powder their noses or whatever else they do, which is a guaranteed act of total acceptance.

In about an hour or two, Rosita and Mike take their leave, for where no one knows, and immediately there is much discussion concerning Rosita, her looks and manners, her southern drawl, and her peculiar resistance to provide anyone with her last name.

Peggy Early goes on at a great rate, as is her right in view of her lofty position in booze joint society, contending that Rosita is defintely a southern belle, probably from Richmond, Virginia, that she no doubt comes from an old and respected southern family and is at least a graduate of a fine southern finishing school. How Peggy gets to deduce all this I cannot understand, but all the other dames in the joint seem to agree so I figure it must be true.

As the conversations drone on, most all of the men in the group make mention that they have all seen her before, but cannot recall where or when and remarks like these seem to please all the female characters.

On each of the two following Thursday nights the whole scenario is repeated with Rosita continuing to intrigue one and all and with Peggy Early playing Zoltan Kaparthy to Mike Murphy's Rosita, as Henry Higgins does to Eliza Doolittle in Shaw's *Pygmalion.*

On the third successive Thursday, Mike appears without the beautiful Rosita and while one and all inquire as to her whereabouts, Mike Murphy is silent as a stone, refusing to provide any information. I find this very peculiar, for Mike is not the kind of guy who lets things get away from him, especially someone as lovely as Rosita. Furthermore I detect a sarcastic smile on his kisser whenever the subject of Rosita and her whereabouts is raised.

Rosita would probably have been forgotten were it not for a peculiar turn of events.

The following Tuesday afternoon, after their usual cocktails, the Ladies of the Schuylkill County Auxiliary, headed by the flamboyant Peggy, visit the Schuylkill County jail and to their utter amazement are confronted with the beautiful Rosita, who is now a blond with short hair. She has left her brunette wig at Big Mary's whorehouse in Park Crest where she and two other lovelies are arrested by the local law on the previous Sunday.

To say that the ladies are aghast is the understatement of the century.

The next time I see Mike Murphy is in the Silver Duck, a Shenandoah drinking establishment, and after reminding him that he owes me a favor, I plead with him to tell me about the beautiful Rosita.

"Well" says Mike, "You are probably aware that I frequent the various county houses of ill repute. Several months ago I come across Rosita in Big Mary's Bordello and I make her a fair proposition, but first I must give you her background. She is not from Richmond, Virginia, but is a native of Harlan County, Kentucky. She is not the daughter of a renowned southern family; her old man is a straw boss in a soft coal mine. She is not a graduate of a fine southern finishing school, but a five year veteran of the prostitution ring which exists between Scranton, Harrisburg and Philadelphia, and she is only twenty-two years old."

"Frankie Motto, the Gilberton white slaver," says Mike, "will pay her fine in a few days and she will be transferred to Harrisburg or even Chicago and she will continue her trade, for she is a real professional, take it from one who knows."

"The proposition I make her," continues Mike, "is simply that I will pay her for her services at the rate of one hundred dollars for each Thursday, it being her day off, and for the aforementioned fee, she will attend the dances at the Lake and the soirees at Sammy Cole's joint and perform other services which are strictly personal to me."

"I do all this," says Mike, "to take Peggy Early and her crew down a rung or two. It was my intention to make Rosita's background known to one and all by word of mouth, although I had not figured out how, but her arrest and the resulting publicity was an easy solution to my problem."

"I wonder," says Mike, "what is going on in some of the Schuylkill County bedrooms and what other repercussions are resulting now that Rosita's secret is out?"

"Because," continues Mike, "every one of the men involved admitted they had seen her before as a blonde."

In the furor that develops in Schuylkill County booze joint society following the revelation of Rosita's profession, several noteworthy things take place.

Ruth Mast sheds herself of Johnny Schmidt like an old glove and takes up with the drama critic of the Philadelphia *Inquirer* who she meets at an affair held for the Schuylkill County Theatre Guild and who, she hopes, will further her career.

Peggy Early, recognizing that discretion is the better part of valor, immediately leaves for an extended trip to Bermuda, paid for by husband Handsome, where she will contemplate what further retribution should be forthcoming from her less than devoted husband. Peggy is joined by her close friend and companion, the lovely Amanda Dawson, who tells Les Hemmerly to go play with his dumb bells.

This is great news to me as I still have my secret yen for Amanda, even though I know in my heart that I am reaching for the moon.

Dottie Wasley of Pottsville is not seen with Bill Mainwaring anymore and rumor has it that Bill may relent and play minor league baseball at Utica, N.Y., in the Phillies' organization.

Joe Kiley and Harry Tierney of Mahanoy City, both ardent Catholics, leave for a "retreat" at Malvern, Pa., where one and all reflect and meditate on their respective life styles and which Joe and Dan hope will reopen the doors to their wives' bedrooms.

Harry Paul stays in Hazleton and does his dancing at Gus Genetti's on Route 309, but not with Jennie Bimot.

Jim McHall of Lansford holes up in the Mahoning Valley Country Club near Lehighton, Pa., leaving Mary Gaughan on her own on her climb up the social ladder.

The entire episode of the beautiful Rosita would have been simply another event in the terrible thirties and everyone would have forgotten her, had it not been for Frank Bellet, the county bank magnate.

About a month later, I am sitting with Honest Pete the gambler in Lou Tendler's booze joint on South Broad Street in Philly and who walks in but Big Jack, Frank's bodyguard. After a few belts of the grog and some urging on my part to tell me why he is in Philly, Big Jack tells me so.

"You may not know," says Big Jack, "but my boss, Mr. Bellet, does many banking favors for Frankie Motto of Gilberton. Not long ago Mr. Bellet asks Frankie to respond in kind and the result is that Rosita is no longer contracted for by Frankie's prostitution ring and will become Mr. Bellet's paid secretary and traveling companion. Mr. Bellet and Rosita are presently across the street in the Bellvue-Stratford, which is much too rich for my blood, and are ironing out the financial arrangements. From the way it appears to me, Rosita will return with us to Mr. Bellet's home in Shenandoah and I will no longer be required to sleep in the same room with him."

"This situation," continues Big Jack, "appears to be of a temporary nature for one of the conditions that Rosita insists upon is that after an agreed on period of time, Mr. Bellet will finance her in her own house of ill repute, somewhere in the Pocono Mountains."

After Big Jack leaves, I tell the whole story to Honest Pete, after which he asks me a peculiar question.

"How far," asks Honest Pete, "are the Poconos from Sammy Cole's?"

"A Second Chance"

IN EARLY SEPTEMBER OF 1939, I am in Philly doing some of my business with Honest Pete, the gambler. We are in attendance at the Merion Cricket Club when the Australian duo of Bromwich and Quist relieve the Americans of the Davis Cup by beating the likes of Frankie Parker, Jack Kramer, and Joe Hunt. Pete has latched on to a Main Line millionaire who in his patriotic zeal wagers one thousand one spots to Pete's five hundred that the Americans will prevail. Everyone knows, at least in Philly, that it turns out that the down-unders are victorious and the Cup takes the long trip to the land of the waltzing matildas.

Pete has scrounged two press badges from a Philadelphia *Bulletin* reporter he knows from Lou Tendler's booze joint on South Broad Street, the possesion of which allows Pete and me to enter the clubhouse and mingle with Philly's bluebloods. These characters, whose pedigrees go back to William Penn, stand alone in their opinion of themselves. Socialites from New York are looked upon as mere upstarts and high brows from Boston are simply tolerated. To the well-born of Philly, nothing exists west of Pittsburg, Pa., and they feel that all Californians should be separated from the union and find a country of their own, which might not be a bad idea.

A description of the characters in attendance is in order, the details of which are related to me from the mouth of one Johnny Leary, who is a waiter in the joint. This Johnny Leary is from Shenandoah, Pa., the only western town in the east, from where he escapes three years ago in search of work in

29

order to keep himself and his everloving in meat and potatoes. Johnny and yours truly attend the J.W. Cooper High School in Shenandoah together in the early thirties and we are old friends. I get to see Johnny most every time I do my business at Connie Mack Stadium for he is a Phillies fan and believes they can do no wrong, which is a distortion of the truth if I have ever heard one.

After Pete and I are seated at a table in a remote corner of the vast edifice, Johnny Leary stations himself close to our location and between his required trips to the bar to secure drinks for other members of the distinguished crowd, he whispers to us many items of interest; however, his first comment is one of absolute amazement to even see us in a joint like this, for the last time he sees me in a booze joint is in a night spot in Shenandoah, Pa. called "The Golden Pheasant," which pales to insignificance when compared to an establishment like the Merion Cricket Club, and is owned and operated by a guy called "The Champ" who once played football for the Pottsville Maroons and the Shenandoah Presidents and is known far and wide as the best night club bouncer in the world.

Johnny tells us that first of all, we are in the wrong attire. All high noses who attend affairs like this are dressed in white jackets with varying colors of vertical stripes. They wear open collar shirts, dark blue trousers, black and white sport shoes and hats which look like baseball caps except that they are emblazoned with the letters M.C.C. The different colored stripes on the jackets denote varied backgrounds. The Philly socialites wear red striped jackets to denote the shedding of their aristocratic blood in all of this country's wars, even before Bunker Hill. The Boston characters wear purple striped jackets to give the impression that they are descended from royalty, but the Philly gentlemen look upon them as nothing more than money-grubbing yankees. The New York individuals wear black stripes to indicate their sorrow for having sacrificed Manhattan and most of the other four boroughs to the millions of immigrants who descended upon the city in the last

30

hundred years. The New York aristocrats eventually emigrate to Connecticut and other out-of-the-way places, but they accomplish this exodus long after the Philly blue bloods have moved to their precious Main Line, proving in Philly at least, that New Yorkers are upstarts and with no forethought.

Also in attendance is the Wilmington, Delaware crowd. These giants of industry wear orange stripes to indicate their hereditary descent from William of Orange, who accepts the British throne after the people of England kick out the Catholic James the Second in 1688. The Philly patricians consider this to be far from the truth, as they know that the only old world family of any importance in Delaware is the Dupont conglomerate, and all of them are French, not Dutch.

The female characters all look alike. They wear tight sweaters, skirts which extend to slightly above the knee, white and brown oxfords and white knee high socks. They are all tanned and extremely healthy looking with blond hair, natural and otherwise, and in contrast with the men, they do not wear a garment which might indicate their birthplace. This proves to me what I have always said, that most female characters will make use of a buck, no matter what bank it comes from.

So you can see that people like yours truly and Honest Pete the gambler are very much out of place when one considers that Pete owns but two suits of clothes which he changes each Christmas and Easter.

It is at this affair that Honest Pete collects his one thousand one spots from a Main Line patrician whose last name is Biddle, and after this takes place, we take our leave, for all this is much too rich for our plebian blood. However, I must comment that I partake of two Bloody Marys while I am there and I confess that I never tasted such wonderful Bloody Marys, even the ones I occasionally imbibe in McGraw's night club in Lost Creek, Pa., which has the reputation for serving the best Bloody Marys in the world.

After we take our leave, we are strolling along the pathways between the many tennis courts and who do I run into but Dr.

Emmet Kistler, the emminent Shenandoah pathologist. The good doctor seems glad to see me and tells me that he has a room with twin beds in the Hotel Philadelphian on Chestnut Street in West Philly and that he would be happy to share the room with me tonite, should I be so inclined. This is music to my ears, as the place I stay the previous evening is a flea bag on Walnut between 12th and 13th Streets and is well known for harboring characters of ill repute.

Suddenly, who comes along but Bruce Evans and his girl friend Babs, from Pottsville Pa., but who are one time residents of the only western town in the east and I begin to think it is some type of a reunion. Never in history have as many as four characters from a place like Schuylkill County been seen in a joint as ritzy as the Merion Cricket Club. After some pleasant conversational exchanges, Bruce and Babs continue on their way and I comment to Dr. Kistler that in as much as Bruce Evans is but a teller in the Industrial Bank in Pottsville and Babs an unemployed post-debutante, it comes as a surprise to me that they can afford the expense of attending an affair like a Davis Cup match, particularly in view of the clothes they are wearing, both being draped in matching cashmere jackets, blue in color, with matching gray flannel slacks, matching suede shoes and matching yellow scarfs. Bab's flannel slacks are tight fitting and with a shape like hers, all the spectators discontinue watching the tennis players and gaze admiringly at Babs, for she is built like Rita Hayworth.

It occurs to me at the time that I am seeing more and more of Bruce and Babs. Being in the gambling profession and operating in and around Schuylkill County, it is my custom to frequent different night spots such as the Green Gables, north of Hazleton, the Amber Lantern in Hometown, and the Bartenders and Waitresses Club in Pottsville, not to mention Cinco's and the Golden Pheasant in Shenandoah, and many other places of interest. When I am in Philly I can usually be found in Lou Tendler's booze joint on South Broad Street, Frank Palumbo's in South Philly, and occasionally in the Hunt

Room at the Bellvue. During the daylight hours, usually after 3:00 P.M., as I do not normally arise until at least 2:00 P.M., I frequent John the Greek's restaurant in Shenandoah, and when in Philly, I conduct my daylight business in Lou Tendler's booze joint.

I frequent these dives because that is where the gambling money hangs out. In my time I make bets on most every kind of action including live pigeon shooting matches, cock fights, all the major sports such as football, baseball, and basketball, and have even won and lost a few wagers on golf. My most peculiar experiment in the gambling dodge is when I play license plate poker with Matt Jupiter, the Pottsville Impressario, for two solid hours in front of that city's celebrated Bartenders and Waitresses Club and break even. For the uninformed, license plate poker is a simple game. Matt would arbitrarily select the third car which is to pass the club going west and I would select the third car going east and whichever plate, letters excluded, having the better poker hand, wins the bet. It is at one time rumored that Matt relieves a hot shot from Scranton of several grand on a rigged game by manipulating the use of several cars with plates showing two pairs and three of a kind, but that is another story. When I make my bets with Matt, I am sure that the caper is not rigged for by doing so, Matt would violate the unwritten law of honesty among professionals.

Well anyway, it seems that no matter what night spot I frequent, I seem to continually run into Bruce and Babs, and when I do, I observe that he is spending money like King Farouk. How he does all this on a teller's salary is beyond me, particularly in view of the fact that he gets from place to place in a new Cadillac convertible.

After they pass by, it is time to leave and I make my farewells to Pete, telling him I will join him at Franklin Field in October when the Penn football season begins.

With Dr. Kistler, I leave the premises in the good doctor's car and proceed to the Philadelphian where after a fine dinner

33

and a few blasts of Benedictine and Brandy, we retire to his room where he tells me the astonishing tale of how on the previous Friday night, at the request of Handsome Early, the Irish undertaker from Shenandoah, Pa. he revives "The Ace" who is being waked by Handsome and Len Sak, the Polish undertaker, in Handsome's funeral parlor and how "The Ace" is not dead at all but just suffering an acute attack of narcolepsy and "The Ace," upon receiving an injection of a drug known to Dr. Kistler alone, returns to consciousness and is none the worse for his experience.

I then tell the Doctor that I myself am in attendance earlier in the evening, but flee the premises in the fear of being arrested for defrauding the public.

The next morning I am awakened by a newsboy on Chestnut Street shouting that terrible word, WAR. I immediately turn on the hotel radio and learn that Hitler invades Poland and Britain and France declare war and that the world will never again be the same as it is on this lovely morning in Philadelphia, Pennsylvania.

But at least for a little while everything seems to remain unchanged. I continue to confine my activities to my profession, doing rather nicely by the way; however, I am more and more concerned about Hitler's success in Europe, and I find myself reading more in the daily blats than the sport pages.

I continue to see Bruce and Babs in the better class rum joints and it seems to me that they are wearing more beautiful clothes and spending more moola than they do in the past.

The straw that breaks the camel's back comes in December of 1940. Honest Pete comes all the way to Shenandoah to alert me to a coming wipeout. It seems that Pete likes the Chicago Bears over the Washington Redskins in the N.F.L. championship game which is to take place in Washington, D.C. on the coming Sunday. Pete is ready to accept Redskins money and allow a gigantic spread of eighteen points to the Skins. He tells me he runs out of moola covering wagers on the Skins and when the word gets around Philly that he is giving eighteen points, he has to escape to Shenandoah as the gamblers are breaking down his door in their eagerness to bet on what they think is a sure thing.

When Pete tells me that the Bears will win by at least thirty points, I am at a loss for words, but I respect his long experience with sure things and I unload my coffers and hock most of my valuables to raise as much as I can and when all the bets are finally made, Pete has about thirty grand and I have about five riding on the Bears.

Before Pete leaves for Philly, he tells me a remarkable thing. His outlet at the Pimlico Race Track in Maryland advises him that a guy from Pottsville named Bruce Evans purchases a promising two year old colt which he names Lucky Bruce and that this nag is a potential Kentucky Derby candidate. Again I am totally amazed at Bruce's buying potential, but I have other things on my mind, such as the Bears-Skins game and the item about Bruce Evans is put aside for the time being.

As everyone knows who follow the important things in life like prize fights, baseball and basketball games, and the National Football League, the story of the Bear-Redskins game of 1940 is still disbelieved by many. Coach George Halas of the Bears, with the help of former Bear Coach Clark Shaughnessy introduces revolutionary changes in the T formation and the Bears go on to win the game by the unbelievable score of seventy-three to nothing. It is even said at the time that with the agreement of both coaches, the game is shortened by seven minutes to keep the score down.

As is easily understood, Pete and I make a killing and later on in Lou Tendler's booze joint I get to ask him how he comes to know that the Bears will unveil the T formation in the slaughter of the Redskins, and even though we are life-long friends and partners in the sting, he refuses to relate his source, saying that he will take it with him to his grave and this I firmly believe.

It is not long after the football game that I see Joe Topton,

35

the editor of the local blat in John the Greek's restaurant in Shenandoah where he tells me that the Feds have lain their claws on Bruce Evans in the Industrial Bank in Pottsville where Bruce's till is short in the amount of one hundred and eight grand. Bruce's father, a member of the bank's board of directors exerts his muscle and the entire episode is kept out of newsprint, with the elder Mr. Evans making good the loss. This, however, does not satisfy the Feds who insist that Bruce spend one year at government expense at the federal penitentiary in nearby Lewisburg, Pa.

Needless to say, I do not see any more of Bruce or Babs around the local night spots, and this is slightly depressing for though I am prone to be leery of dames, feeling that all dames spell trouble, a shape like Babs' would be missed anywhere, even in Hollywood, Calif.

Suddenly comes Pearl Harbor and after not many months I receive my greetings from F.D.R. and am practically dragged to the induction center in New Cumberland, Pa. where various imbeciles prod and grill me to find out what use they can make of my body. They know, and I don't know how, that when I am very young and with the Depression at its height, I am employed as a telegram delivery boy by Western Union and in my spare time I learn the Morse Code, and with my good physical condition, thanks to my daily constitutionals on the Shenandoah Pike, these imbeciles decide that they will make a radio-operator gunner out of me and put me in a B-24 Liberator bomber. When I protest and say that I have never been in an airplane in my life and if left alone will never do so and that furthermore I am not mad at anyone and no one is mad at me, at least to my knowledge, it is to no avail and after a period of rigorous training I find myself twenty thousand feet in the air over such out of the way places as Vienna, Austria; Munich, Germany; Ploesti, Rumania; and Prague, Czechoslovakia being shot at by individuals in Messerschmidt 109s, Focke-Wolf 190s, and by The Marshall Goering elite anti-aircraft gunners, all of whom are trying to kill me even

36

though I do not know them, have never seen them, and whom I would never disturb had things stayed the same as they were in Shenandoah, Pa. during the thirties, when one and all continually griped about the Depression. But all that is another story.

It comes to the Christmas season of 1944 and I am on my way to a combat crew rest camp on the Isle of Capri and am laying over in the city of Naples, Italy, and while sitting at a table in the Galleria, a glass-covered edifice shielding restaurants, shops, drug stores and so forth, in the European manner, and while enjoying an Italian espresso, who do I see strolling through the Galleria but Bruce Evans of Pottsville, Pa. I immediately hail Bruce to join me in an espresso for though I am but a Technical Sergeant and he is a First Lieutenant, I do not believe in the separation of Officers and enlisted men, for Officers put their pants on one leg at a time and perform their bodily functions just as I do.

Bruce is of the same stripe, being of Schuylkill County, Pa., and we enjoy an afternoon interlude in the Galleria where Bruce imparts to me his amazing story.

"After I am relieved of my responsibilities at the Lewisburg Pen," says Bruce, "I do not return to Pottsville as my reputation has dropped lower than the stock market in '29. I immediately offer my services to the U.S. Army and even though I have a record, they accept me at once for as you well know, in 1942 the armed services will accept anyone, blind, deaf, or crippled. When I am accepted, and with my experience in banking, I am assigned to the Finance Department and at first do nothing but clerical work in Rome. As for the war," says Bruce Evans, "I am safer here than I am in Pottsville, for there I might be run over by some drunk in a car. I have not seen any combat and I'm sure I never will and I must tell you that when I see the wings on your chest and the ribbon indicating the Distinguished Flying Cross, I feel for you greatly for I know you have done nothing to the Germans that would cause them to use you for a clay pigeon."

"One evening in Rome," says Bruce Evans, "I am at an officers' bash in the Victoria Hotel and am standing at the bar next to a Colonel with a pronounced Philadelphia accent and I take a chance and say as follows. 'Excuse me sir, could it be that you are from Philly?' 'Absolutely,' says the Colonel. 'My name is Cadwalader Duke and I am from Merion, Pa.' This," says Bruce Evans, "leads to a long conversation about Philly and its environs and when I tell him that the last time I am in Philly it is to see Adrian Quist and John Bromwich remove the Davis Cup from the possession of the Americans at the Merion Cricket Club in 1939, he nearly falls over." He tells me that he is there as well and that back in Merion, Pa., his white jacket with red stripes is hanging in his closet and will be used again at the first opportunity.

"One thing leads to another," says Bruce Evans, "and the good Colonel sees to it that I am transferred to his staff here in Naples, where I am assigned to the payroll department of the entire Mediterranean Theater of Operations."

"Instead of the measly million or so that I am exposed to in the Bank in Pottsville, Pa.," says Bruce Evans, "here I handle billions, and with what I learn from the expert bank manipulators when I am in college at the Lewisburg Pen, there is no limit to my advancement, now that I have a second chance."

After Lt. Evans leaves, I sit back and think the whole thing through and I come to the conclusion that when he becomes a millionaire, and he most certainly will, it is my hope that he will always have his beautiful Babs at this side, that he will always have his fine taste for the better things in life and just possibly, some day, he might even put on an all-white jacket with red stripes, too.

"A Round to Remember"

IT WAS THE TIME of the great 52/20 club and there was rejoicing in our land the equal of which had never been seen before and more than likely would never be seen again, for World War Two had come to an end.

There were celebrations in every city, town, and hamlet in this great land and yes, beyond the seas, where every race, color, and creed of our globe took time to raise a glass in thanks to a God, who in the minds of many, should never have allowed the immense slaughter to occur in the first place.

But there was universal rejoicing and the sorrows and pains of the last seven years were for the time forgotten, for this is human nature.

Brahmins in India and Junkers in Prussia, Lords in England and Commissars in Russia, Shieks in Arabia and Roués in France, Imperialists in Japan and Tribal Chiefs in Africa as well as Landlords in Ireland and Gentry in Australia all mingled with the common people of their native lands imbibing and carousing and finally recognizing that though the high noses had begun the whole affair, it was left to the world's middle and lower classes to settle the issue.

And the middle and lower classes celebrated as well. Coal miners in Wales and Taxi drivers in Paris, factory workers in Leningrad and bus boys in Hawaii, coolies in China and peasants in Bavaria, Eskimos in Alaska and spear wielding blacks in the Congo as well as farmers in Australia and Basques in Spain all nearly went mad with joy coming to the conclusion that after Hiroshima and Nagasaki, there could be no more wars, high noses' greed for power and prestige not withstanding.

But of all the celebrations world wide, none even approached what happened in the United States of America from August 1945 to August 1946, and this year long period of absolute pandemonium was the result of the 52/20 club.

For the uninformed, the 52/20 club worked as follows. Honorably discharged veterans who did not have a job to return to and those who did have jobs but for justifiable reasons of their own, chose to take a year's sabbatical and say to hell with going to work, were, at the expense of the U. S. Government, provided with twenty dollars each week for fifty-two consecutive weeks.

This action perpetuated the greatest year long bash in the history of mankind and no area in the United States celebrated in greater fashion than Schuylkill County in Pennsylvania.

Gin mills such as Large George's and Eddie Paskov's in Shenandoah, Scrimey Liebacov's and Red Rut's in Mahanoy City, the Nineteenth St. Cafe and the Brass Rail in Pottsville, Scrafford's in Hometown and McGraw's in Lost Creek and many, many more throughout the county were packed to the rafters day and night, with no closing time.

There were war stories upon war stories, tales of heroism and cowardice, of loyalty and of sedition, of joy and sorrow with the quantity and quality of the tales increasing proportionately to the amount of booze consumed.

In my line of work I am required to frequent gin mills for I am a gambler by profession and booze joints are where the gambling money hides out. I figured that in the period of August to August beginning in 1945, I heard just about every war story ever told and I am none the worse for the telling for these G.I.s had looked eyeball to eyeball with the grim reaper and have lived to tell about it. But it is not my intention to tell war stories, though someday I may, God willing, and might even tell a few about myself, for even yours truly who despises violence in any form and should know better, at one time

40

played clay pigeon for the Marshall Goering elite group of anti-aircraft gunners 24,000 feet over Vienna and even fired a Browning 50 caliber machine gun at ME-262 jet fighters over Munich, flown by the likes of General Adolph Galland, a high nose in the Luftwaffe, at a time when the most advanced country in the world did not have a jet fighter even on a drawing board. But all that is another story.

During this period and in my travels I encountered many citizens with whom I consorted before the big war and there was much joy at our reunions.

For one, there was Bill Mainwaring of Pottsville, the talented first baseman of the Pine Grove Athletics who in 1941 was to play for the Philadelphia Phillies but instead wound up as a Captain in the 101st Airborne Division and was present at Bastogne when General MacAulife made his immortal reply of "Nuts."

I ran into Bill at the Nineteenth St. Cafe in Pottsville in late November of 1945, where I had a mark who laid five hundred one spots against my four hundred that the Washington Redskins would defeat the Cleveland Rams in the National Football League championship game on the following Sunday.

Bill is a most demonstrative guy and can be heard in the next block even when he thinks he is whispering and I had to place my bad ear next to him as the noise level was all but intolerable.

We spoke of many things, the great days of the dances at Lakewood Park in Barnesville, the Pottsville Maroons and the Shenandoah Presidents, but it seemed we always reverted to the topic of mutual friends who didn't come out of the war. He told me that Jack Barry, the shoe salesman of Pottsville was blown to bits in a B-24 over Ploesti and I replied that Johnny Demanich, the beer distributor of Shenandoah fell before a Schmieser machine pistol at Anzio. And so it goes.

All this tended to morbidity and we made a special effort to look ahead, trying our best to forget the damn war.

Just then, who came through the door but Bobby Glendower and I was absolutely shocked when I saw him. This Bobby Glendower was a Shenandoah native, one or two generations removed, is now a resident of Pottsville and is, and has always been, a little guy. He is about five feet four inches tall and weighs about one hundred and twenty-five pounds but all of it is, and always was, packed with dynamite. He is of Welsh descent, his family name claiming direct descent from the Welsh hero, Owen Glendower, who in the fourteenth century in a revolt against the English usurper, Henry the Fourth, provided the nation of Wales with a hero figure far greater in the Welsh mind than Arthur of England or St. Patrick of Ireland.

What shocked me when I saw him was the fact that he seemed to be smaller and thinner than I had remembered. While I had become rather used to war casualties, such as missing arms and legs, to see one as emaciated as Bobby Glendower was frightening.

Bobby had been a golf nut and played and scored well in pro-am tournaments all over the state. To watch the little guy split fairways with two hundred and thirty yard drives, hit short irons and wedges like Ben Hogan, and almost always sink the ten to fifteen foot putt made slobs like myself stick to throwing darts in gin mills or playing two hand klob with guys like Large George, the Shenandoah bar room impressario.

This was the first time I had seen him since 1941, but I was aware of his wartime exploits. I knew he had become a Lieutenant in Merril's Marauders in the China-Burma-India theatre, spending at least three years in Burma, a God forsaken area, and among the many things he collected was malarial dysentery, one of the cruelest diseases ever to afflict mankind.

To say that Bobby Glendower was emaciated was not to do him justice. His eyes were sunken and his pre-war sweater hung over his frame like a Ringling Brother's tent. His hands and face had a yellowish hue and he had a pronounced limp, favoring his left leg. As he moved to the bar and stood next to Bill Mainwaring, the contrast was all but frightening.

Big Bill, who is about as dignified as a kick in the groin, greeted him with, "Hi ya Bobby, where did they leave the rest of you?" To which Bobby replied, "Most of it is in Rangoon, but part of me is still floating in the Irrawaddy; bowel movements come quick and often in that part of the world."

Though this type of repartee might sound abrasive to the average listener, it was the style of banter heard in most of the gin mills in the country, for the G.I.'s found this type of macabre humor self-serving, laughing at themselves and the situations they had been placed in and not by their own choosing.

To laugh in the face of adversity seems to be a peculiar British and American characteristic, but there are limits to everything. Though Bill, and even yours truly, might joke about how gaunt and wasted Bobby might appear, the subject of golf was not brought up.

There was no doubt in my mind that it would be a long time, if ever, that Bobby Glendower would once again split a fairway with a two hundred and thirty yard drive but this lack of accomplishment paled in comparison when I thought of the blind, the amputees, and the mental wrecks that were evident everywhere during the great celebration at the time of the 52/20 club.

But sadness and remorse over lost limbs and sight, incurable physical and mental illness were the exception rather than the rule and the joy of seeing and celebrating with old friends, who had somehow persevered, was by far the prevailing mood.

When Bobby Glendower left the Nineteenth St. Cafe, I went with him. All the jovial hi-jinks aside, he appeared lost in thought. I had always admired him for his tenacity and self-endurance in view of his slight stature, but it was easy to deduce that he seemed sad and philosophical.

We walked south on Nineteenth St. to Mahantongo St. and he told me that while in Burma he had come across a copy of John O'Hara's *Appointment in Sammara* and had read it several times and on each occasion thought more and more of the time of his return and now he was home.

"Here, all around me," he said, "is O'Hara's Gibbsville. Here is *Appointment in Samarra* and down the street is the Gibbsville Club. I can almost feel the presence of the ghost of Julian English wandering up and down Mahantongo St. searching in vain for his beloved Caroline. Where does Luke Fleeger live? He who loved sex in the early morning. Here is the heart of that portion of the state of Pennsylvania turned into a legendary menage of waspish tycoons and Irish romantics by the son of an upper middle class Irish doctor, who by his own admission told the truth better than anyone else about his time, the first half of the twentieth century."

"Where," said Bobby, "are all the members of the second Thursday club where admission is gained only through the death of one of its members, the prospective inductee being screened by a committee which oversaw the applicant's lineage and financial position but more importantly his social position and behaviour as compared with the standards of the time? It was almost like being named to Great Britain's Knight of the Garter."

"What happened," he said, "to Froggy who lost an arm at Belleau Wood and where are all the sad faces of the Pottsvillians lost in the two great wars?"

"Gibbsville boys, Pottsville boys if you will," said Bobby, "always came to glorious deaths in the wars. Pottsville boys died clean shaven, plunging to their deaths in flaming P-38 fighter planes over Truk or in a B-24, blown to bits over Vienna. They died on aircraft carriers or in submarines beneath the sea. This is how O'Hara would have them die for sure."

At this time I reminded Bobby that I was a native of Shenandoah, Pottsville's neighbor to the north, twelve miles away, a so-called grim place where smoke from a subterranean fire can be seen within a ten minute walk from the borough hall.

"Pottsville to Shenandoah," I said to Bobby, "is New York to Pittsburgh with the inevitable feeling of superiority on the one hand and resentment on the other."

"Shenandoah boys died in the mud of Normandy," I said, "or were bayoneted in the belly by a Japanese infantry man on Guadalcanal."

"There is no such thing in Shenandoah as the second Thursday club, only the Elks and the Eagles. Pottsvillians always demeaned Shenandoah's Snow Dance on New Year's eve in Maher's hall when compared to their own annual Assembly in the same night in Pottsville's Necho Allen Hotel."

"I remember a guy from Shenandoah who was courting a Pottsville girl saying that she was so refined, so sweet and demure that he couldn't imagine her having a bowel movement."

Bobby howled.

After leaving Bobby at his home, I returned to the Nineteenth St. Cafe where the usual afternoon booze session was in progress.

Fritz Dorfman, recently discharged as a tank commander in Patton's Third Army, who had left his two year old palomino in the capable hands of Johnny Clark, the Orwigsburg farmer back in 1942, was reunited with his beautiful horse and while under the influence was trying to ride the horse through the front door of the cafe. His entrance was barred by Paul Clewell, the former radio operator of the submarine Skate, who was throwing lighted fire crackers at the horse's feet.

Fritz rode roughshod over these insignificant impediments, entered the cafe, tied the horse to a wall coat hanger, and ordered a shot and a beer. Everyone but Joe Newell, the partially deaf bartender, who was too old to be taken in the service, ran out the back door showing that he had more raw courage than all the so-called war heros combined.

After Fritz downed his shot and a beer, he casually mounted

45

and rode out, bound for Johnny Gratz's gin mill on West Market St., where he said he would repeat his performance.

Episodes like this were prevalent all over Schuylkill County, and the constabulary turned a closed eye and a deaf ear to such insignificant pranks.

And there were arguments galore. Bill Mainwaring of the 101st Airborne Division almost came to blows with Peanuts McGuire of the First Marine Division over which was the tougher outfit. Bernard Dawson, the utility heir and brother to the lovely Amanda who is my secret yen, and who recently returned after chasing Rommel all over North Africa and who was but a private, threatened to destroy his brother Eddie, the recently returned deck officer of the USS Missouri, when Eddie told him that the Navy was the one and only branch of the service.

But as all things will, the 52/20 club came to an end and unfortunately many of the G.I.'s, not used to daily drinking, ended as alcoholics, with thousands of them dying in their late forties or fifties from acute alcoholism, various illnesses affecting the liver, permanent brain damage, and other alcohol-induced maladies.

So many of my friends went this route. George Straghn of Shenandoah, a hero of the First Marine Division on Guadalcanal, succumbed to the booze in 1958. George, who seemed impervious to Jap bullets in two island invasions as a marine, died little more than a vegetable in a Veteran's hospital in Lebanon.

Harry Mahaffey, also of Shenandoah, a gunnery officer on a destroyer in the Aleutian campaign and who lost an arm at Attuck, succumbed to the booze in 1959, and many, many more also died.

I did not see Bobby Glendower again until 1950 in Williamsport, Pa. My business had grown over the years and I found that people will bet on an inside straight or on athletic events from their hearts, rather than their heads, in places other than Schuylkill County and Philadelphia, Pennsylvania.

In Williamsport, at the Lycoming Hotel bar, I listened on the radio to the final game of the National League season with a mark who had laid me one thousand to my seven hundred that the Brooklyn Dodgers would persevere and capture the pennant.

As my friend Honest Pete the Philly gambler had predicted, Robin Roberts of the Phillies pitched a masterpiece and Dick Sisler hit the home run in the tenth inning that turned the city of Philadelphia into a delirious state and made me a bit richer. So later on that afternoon, when Bobby walked into the bar, I bought him a drink.

He still limped, which seemed more pronounced, but other than that he seemed to look better. Most of the yellowish hue had left him, but he was still ungodly thin. However, he had obviously improved emotionally. He was no longer subdued, seemed considerably more outgoing, and had much more to say.

We spoke at length of the wild days in Schuylkill County in 1946 at first, but later on he told of what had happened to him since then.

He had married a nurse whom he had met while in India and who had taken care of him during his battle with malarial dysentery. She was a Williamsport native and shortly after their marriage in 1946, they took an apartment in that city. A little girl was born in 1948 whom they curiously named India, after the country in which they had met.

Unfortunately, the union was not firm. His wife, Sue, was prone to be impatient with his moody depressions. He would regularly retreat within himself, not speaking to her for weeks at a time. In a short time, in 1949 to be exact, they were divorced and Bob lived alone, which surprisingly seemed to bolster his spirits. It was at this time of his life that I met him at the Lycoming Hotel.

He was employed by the Breyers Ice Cream Co. of Philadelphia as local sales manager and still seemed to spend freely, which had always been one of his characteristics.

47

For reasons that I will never understand, Bobby always opened his heart and his innermost thoughts to me. It might have been because I was a little older, that we were veterans of a cruel war, and that we were born and raised in the same area, but I will never really know.

As the years went by I saw less and less of Bobby, my business diminishing in the Central Pennsylvania area, but one night in 1959 I ran into him at the bar of the Edison Hotel in Sunbury, Pa. He had his new wife with him. She was at least five feet ten inches in height with a wonderful figure, about ten years younger than Bobby, and was the Central Pennsylvania Women's Amateur Golf Champion. She had competed with golfers of the caliber of Helen Seigel Wilson of Philadelphia and Virginia Dyson of Hazleton, Pa., both ranked among the top women amateurs in the state.

She was very attractive and seemed to be the right medicine for Bobby as his demeaner had improved considerably.

After a night of heavy drinking and reminiscing, I was invited to stay overnight at their home and about three A.M. was treated to a remarkable sight. Bobby had fallen asleep on the davenport and Helen calmly and with little exertion, picked him up and carried him to their bedroom, undressed him and placed him safely in bed with what seemed to me, to be the slightest effort.

With Bobby asleep, I learned from Helen that no matter how much she pleaded with him, he would not play a round of golf, contending that with his pronounced limp and lack of his former strength, he could not in any way score in the low seventies, which had been in accordance with his scratch handicap, and that if he could not score as he had before the war, he would not play at all. Helen told me that he still loved the game, attending all of her matches, but was adamant about not playing himself.

As the years went by I saw less and less of Bobby and Helen and this tale might not have been written except for a letter I received many yeas later that read as follows:

48

DEAR F. N. G.,

We extend to you a most urgent invitation to attend Bobby's coming out party. At long last he has agreed to play golf with me, but only on the condition that you are in attendance. I sincerely hope you will come as it means so very much to me.

What has brought this about is that on last February 22, Bob had his left leg amputated at a joint considerably above the knee and he feels that with a handicap such as this, he cannot expect to play as he had when he was younger and will be satisfied if he breaks 90.

In fairness to both of us, I feel compelled to tell you of our relationship leading up to the amputation.

I met Bob in 1954, and after a three year courtship, we were married in July 1957. He was always charming, always a gentleman, holding my coat, opening car doors, lighting my cigarettes. He never said a harsh word to me or to anyone in my presence. He was like no one I had ever gone out with or my mother had ever seen. She loved him too.

He was always very active and always a devilish mischievious fellow, loved to hunt, fish and water ski, but would not play golf.

This all stopped in 1970 when he began to have pains in his left leg. We went to a Christmas party at the Edison Hotel in Sunbury and Dr. George Harwood noticed his pronounced limp. He told Bob that he had a circulatory problem and he should see Dr. Thomas Barrett at Geisinger Medical Center in Danville. The next week Bob met with Dr. Barrett and he was advised he had a blockage in his lower abdomen and needed surgery.

He had his aorta removed and cleaned and an artificial artery (on his next entry to the hospital) placed in his right leg. Again he felt relatively good for a few years and then, more surgery. It was so frustrating.

In August 1979, Bob suffered a blood clot in his left groin, his left leg became very weak, and he suffered much pain. He went to State College and underwent the same surgery. His chest looked like a road map. They inserted artificial arteries from his shoulder to his abdomen four different times. In October, after many of these operations, he pleaded with the doctor to amputate his foot. The doctor still insisted he could save it and told him that he would be active again in the spring.

It did improve a little and Bob could walk on it, until Christmas 1979, when the pain became unbearable. His foot was black and he was discharged from the State College Hospital at his insistence. He was going mad there. He was home from Thursday until Monday, and those days and nights were a nightmare.

I watched him day and night. He sat on the couch many times and picked imaginary things off his clothes. He smoked and fell asleep, burned the carpet, mattress, and his clothes. With Doctor Barrett in Florida at the time, I called his assistant, Dr. Jordan, and told him that Bob was on his "last leg" and I sincerely believed he was. He had lost much weight, wouldn't eat because of the pain, and said that I should admit him the next day, which I did. At the hospital, Dr. Raub assured him he was not going to die and that on Sunday or Monday he would remove his leg. Bob was still taking drugs and suffering like no one I had ever seen.

Saturday afternoon Dr. Jordan came to his room and said "Bob, I don't have anything to do this afternoon, why don't we take your leg off?" Bob said, "Fine, the sooner the better."

THEN THE AMPUTATION. I was so relieved when he returned to his room and the doctor explained how far up he cut to be sure no gangrene was possible. His foot and leg had developed gangrene at State College and had existed for a week before they had agreed to amputate. Both doctors at Williamsport expressed regrets that Bob had waited so long, asking why the other doctors hadn't operated long before they did.

On February 23rd, I thought Bob would suffer a shock when he woke up and saw his leg missing, but he took it as though he had lost a fingernail. He said that very day that he would be active again by May and he was.

After five days, he came home from the hospital, had a big steak at the country club for lunch, and ate a huge dinner that night at home. We were all relieved that it was over.

He now has a prosthesis, which he had fitted in May and walks with a cane. My only fear is that the arteriosclerosis will strike again in another area and he may lose his other leg. I know he thinks of it too. But we don't talk about that—live for today is the theory for us both.

At 10:00 A.M. on Monday, September 1, 1980, he will play his first round of golf since 1941. It will take place at the Susquehanna Valley Country Club. He wants you there and I know you won't disappoint him.

Love,

Helen.

How could I have refused?

I took the whole Labor Day weekend off, arriving at their home on Sunday night. It was a grand reunion.

Their home is adjacent to the fairway of the first hole on the course, so we had not very far to travel.

We went off in two carts, Bob and me with our clubs in one and Helen and her friend Ruth in the other. Bob was determined to break 90, which meant he would have to average five shots a hole. We both knew he would have trouble on the long par fives and that he must score well on the par threes.

The Number one hole was a 380 yard, par 4, straight away, with two yawning traps guarding an elevated green. He topped his tee shot and I was afraid he'd walk off the course. The ball traveled only about 125 yards, but it went down the middle of the fairway. He then hit a three wood, fifty yards from the pin in front of the green. He wedged on and two putted for a five. So far so good. The second hole was a dog leg, 503 yard, par 5. He hit a fairly good tee shot, then slightly topped a three wood, hit another wood to the left of the green, and two putted for a six.

On the short par four No. 3 hole, he had his first par, sinking a ten footer in the process. On Hole No. 4, a par three, he hit a beautiful eight iron, 20 feet from the pin, but took two putts to get down, scoring his second par. He had fives on the next three par 4 holes, took a fat 7 on No. 8, a tough 510 yard, par 5 monster and stood on No. 9 tee with a 40. He hooked his tee shot on No. 9 but it was in his favor as the hole was a dog leg to the left, hit a five iron about 130 yards to the green and two putted for a par. He had made 44 on the front nine, Helen had a 37, and I won't publish my score.

By this time he had collected a considerable gallery, which, knowing the circumstances, cheered every shot. He didn't seem to be tired, but I noticed that he grimmaced each time he swung, particularly when he hit a wood or a long iron.

Helen suggested that he take a slight rest and have a drink, but he insisted on finishing the round.

He took a six on the long par 4 tenth, again topping a fairway wood. It was easy to discern that the old grooved swing was still there, but his timing was off, which could be expected. He made five on the tough par 4 11th and stood on the tee of the par 3 No. 12 and told me he was about ready to make a run at par. He did better than that. He hit a six iron stiff to the pin and sank a four footer for his first birdie. The uphill par 5, 525 yard 13th took its toll. He made six, but only by dropping a twenty foot putt. He made fives on the par 4, 14th and 15th, but seemed to be tiring and I told him he had proved himself and that we should return to the clubhouse.

With the short par 3, 16th, the next hole, he told me to shut up and promptly birdied the hole from eight feet. He took a five on the par 4, 17th and walked up to the 18th tee with a 36.

No. 18 was par 4, a 470 yard monster, the No. 1 handicap hole on the course. He hit his best drive of the day, at least 215 yards, right down the middle, which must be considered long for a one legged guy who hadn't played in forty years. He spanked a three wood, stopping the ball just in front of a creek which crosses the fairway, guarding the green. He wedged to ten feet and made the putt for a par 4. He had made a 40 on the tough back side and added to his 44 on the front side he had a total of 84. A remarkable accomplishment.

Helen picked him up bodily and kissed him on the forehead. The crowd cheered and cheered.

There is very little left to tell of the saga of Bobby Glendower, but one more thing must be told.

The very last thing that Bobby Glendower said to me as I left went as follows:

"IF I SHOULD LOSE MY OTHER LEG, I'LL HAVE ANOTHER ONE FITTED TO ME AND I'LL HAVE YOU BACK TO WATCH ME BREAK 75."

I have been a steely eyed, hard fisted gambler all my life, a student of Honest Pete the Philly gambler, who taught me never to bet from my heart but only with my head, but one bet I will never take would be that Bobby Glendower would not break 75, whether he had but one leg or no legs at all.

Uncle Christopher

OF ALL THE PEOPLE I have known during my tenure on this earth, none that I knew was more intriguing to me that my Uncle Christopher. Actually he was my Grand Uncle, being a brother to my Grandmother, Bridget Franey. His last name was Ferguson and he stemmed from an honored Irish family that is traceable back to Fergus, a member of the Court of Conchobor, King of Ireland in the eleventh century. It is also believed that two Ferguson men, his ancestors, and twin brothers no less, died at the hands of the English while fighting for the Catholic cause at the battle of the Boyne in 1690.

I was a lad of ten when I first laid eyes on him and he was a sight one could never forget. At the time he was seventy four years young, stood six feet, three inches tall, walked perfectly erect and had long flowing white hair, which when he ventured out in the elements was always covered by a large white 10 gallon Stetson. He wore pure leather boots and form fitting coats and trousers and he looked like Buffalo Bill Cody, but Cody was never as handsome as my Uncle Christopher.

For years prior to meeting him, I had attentively listened to stories about him, told to me by my Grandmother. The stories were so interesting that even in my youth I thought them too far fetched to be believed, but after one glimpse of Uncle Christopher, I lost all my doubts completely.

From what I could gather from my Grandmother, he was a great spender and bon vivant. Work to him was anathema, and he felt that in the exciting world he had been placed he would spend all his waking hours in the pursuit of pleasure and adventure.

He was born in 1855 and up to his twenty-fourth birthday had not wanted for anything, being a son of one of the wealthy pioneer families of Shenandoah, Pennsylvania. His prowess as a horseman was widespread and he had won many match races through his younger years with horses he stabled at his cousin Michael O'Hara's farm. He had taken a "Grand Tour" at his parents' expense and was most exemplary in gentlemanly behavior.

Christopher was one of a large family made up of five brothers and two sisters. His sister Bridget, my Grandmother, had married into the Franey family of Shenandoah, Pa., which was one of the first families to settle in the Anthracite Coal region of Pennsylvania.

He had a brother with the unusual name of Fergus Ferguson who died in his early twenties from the results of an injury while playing the new American game of football. Fergus was an undergraduate at an Ivy League University and his family sometimes ruefully claimed that he was the first American to lose his life in this typically American sport.

Christopher's other brothers followed the conventional road to success. One became a prominent attorney, the other two became outstanding businessmen after attending Penn., Harvard, and Yale respectively. The remaining daughter married into another Irish Catholic family in the area.

Christopher was the only one of the children who did not go to college. While he never talked much about it, I got the impression that he felt attending a college or university would be a waste of his precious time. After my father died (when I was twelve) and I had come to rely on Uncle Christopher's judgment, he constantly urged me to take advantage of my Grandmother's extensive library, which fortunately I did. I believe he had read every book in the library and urged me to do the same. He could speak on any subject intelligently, which to him was the mark of true learning.

As told to me by my Grandmother, an event took place in the summer of 1875 which shook Christopher and his family to their very foundations. A local girl lodged a paternity suit in the County Court House, stating that she had been forcibly raped by a group of young men, one of whom she claimed was my Uncle Christopher. While the suit was thrown out of court for insufficient evidence, the resulting scandal so affected Christopher and his family that he left home and in the spring of 1876 he entered the U.S. Army, being attached to a Cavalry Unit at Fort Riley, Kansas. For some unknown reason he wrote only to his sister Bridget and though the letters were infrequent, she was at least able to keep some record of his whereabouts and activities.

According to my Grandmother, he saw action in four skirmishes against the Sioux, being wounded once, suffering an arrow in his left leg above the knee. He eventually spent three hitches of six years each in the cavalry, and sometime during the late 1890's his letters stopped coming. It was reported at one time that he had been promoted to the rank of corporal, but success in achieving rank was not his reason for military service. He was so imbued with the spirit of adventure that remaining a lowly trooper was all that he desired.

Sometime during the winter of 1897, his mother died and not more than two weeks later, his father followed, dying of what contemporaries said was a broken heart.

Attempts were made by the family to located him through the channels of the U.S. Army, but the only shred of evidence uncovered was that he had been honorably discharged at the Army base in Yuma, Arizona on August 18, 1894.

His family contracted with the renowned Pinkerton Detective Agency in an effort to locate him and after a period of approximately two years, they found him living with an Indian squaw in a settlement outside of Albequerque, New Mexico.

When he was notified that he had inherited his portion of

56

his father's imposing estate, he returned to Shenandoah where he tried the life of a retired country gentleman. When the clock struck midnight, December 31, 1899, he entered the twentieth century at the age of 45, with several lifetimes of experiences behind him, but he became bored with the inactivity and resumed his nomadic ways.

In 1901 he set out to travel, and travel he did. He maintained residences for short periods of time in London, Dublin, Edinburgh, and Cardiff in the Isles and Paris, Vienna, and Rome on the continent. He became fluent in French and Italian and over a period of approximately twenty-four years, he returned to Shenandoah on but one occasion.

In 1926 he gave all this up and came home to stay and it was in that year that I first saw him.

In the passing years, Christopher became known for his extensive charity work. He was especially helpful to the unfortunate transients who could be found each day at the Reading Railroad freight yards. Excluding his extravagant tastes in clothes and his love of Irish whiskey, he had nothing else to do with his money, the bulk of which found its way to all types of local charities.

My Uncle Christopher's charity sometimes followed peculiar roads. I remember an incident which might describe it. One day he came upon a young neighborhood boy gazing into the window of a novelty store which displayed a large amount of baseball equipment. This was long before the advent of Little League baseball and most juvenile teams used equipment that was passed from one brother to the next. It was obvious to my Uncle that the boy was dreaming of owning such a collection of sporting gear, large enough to equip a team of nine players. These bats, balls, gloves and catcher's mitts were the prizes to be gained on a punch board, the winning numbers on the board indicating what piece of equipment the lucky player would win. He escorted the boy inside and took some chances on the punch board but won nothing. Later, after the boy left, he took more chances, again won nothing, and finally purchased all the remaining punches on the board and that evening had the entire collection of baseball equipment sent to the boy's home. He probably could have purchased the equipment for less money at a sporting goods store, but he never gave it a thought.

In great secrecy, he saw to it that the male child resulting from the scandal of 1875 received enough money to guarantee his education, all unknown even to his sister Bridget. I was made aware of this years later when a certain area physician related to me that his education had been paid for by my Uncle Christopher. This doctor eventually was assigned to the staff of the St. Agnes Hospital in Philadelphia and became renowned for his ability as an abdominal surgeon.

During his later years, Uncle Christopher lived in my Grandmother's enormous home in Shenandoah. The building still stands today and is so large that after the old people died, it was first made into a hotel and even now functions as the largest apartment house in the town. At its height, the house had a music room, a billiard room, a grand foyer, a hall used for dancing, a large library, ten bedrooms, and five baths. There was an array of servants including a man who functioned as chauffeur and maintanence man, a cook, and two maids, all of whom lived on the premises.

When my father died, my mother and my two brothers moved into the home and it was my good fortune to have a bedroom next to my Uncle Christopher. I sat by the hour both in his bedroom and in the library, as he told of his past experiences and of what he thought the future would bring. There were nights when we would retire to the library and read and talk halfway through the night and on occasion we would both fall asleep in our chairs to be awakened by the servants in the morning. I was often chastised by my mother for this type of behavior, but I shall never forget those nights. I remember reading in their entirety Ridpath's *History of the World*, Gibbon's *Decline and Fall*, the complete works of Sir Walter Scott,

Sir Arthur Conan Doyle, Alfred Lord Tennyson, and most of Shakespeare. History fascinated me, particularly the history of England and Wales, Scotland and Ireland and all that I learned was not necessarily from the books, as Uncle Christopher provided details of events regarding these countries which were not in recorded history but passed by word of mouth from one generation to the next. It was on one night in the library that he told me the story of the battle of the Boyne, that I have previously mentioned, where the red headed Ferguson twins died in the Catholic cause of the Stuart King James II against the Protestant forces of William of Orange. It seems ironic that to this day the same religious feud still persists.

But of all the fascinating things that he told me of, there was none more interesting than his description of an event that took place back in the early nineteenth century in Philadelphia. It did not involve him in a personal way, but had an effect on his sister and her family. It is referred to as the "Franey Legend" which the reader may believe or not.

The legend tells that the original James J. Franey, father-in-law to my Grandmother Bridget, left a pregnant wife and six daughters in County Mayo in the 1820's to seek fame and fortune in the New World. In the true sense of the word he did not leave them destitute, for he was a landed squire who enjoyed a comfortable income for that time and place, but he dreamed of the unlimited heights of success that awaited him in America. The story relates that Mr. Franey, after a short time in the new land, received a letter from his wife telling him that he had become the father of a healthy son, and he immediately forwarded sufficient money to allow his family to join him in Philadelphia.

Several weeks later, Mr. Franey met his family at dockside in Philadelphia and in the ensuing confusion it was noticed that one of the six daughters could not be found. She was four years old and her name was Agnes. She was never heard from again. Mr. Franey and his family were saddened by by their loss, but he was so enthralled by his new son that he was reported to have said, "What's one daughter to me now that I have a son and heir."

As you can see, this was truly an age when real values were confused with the centuries old axiom that only the male children were important and that daughters were useful only to secure a marriage that would improve the lot of the father.

I have often wondered about the lost daughter and pondered the fact that I might have blood relatives living in the Philadelphia area.

It was said at the time and continued to be said in the years that followed that if Agnes Franey had the strength of character and determination of her father, she probably became the wife of a Main Line millionaire, but who will ever know?

Agnes Franey was not necessarily forgotten following her disappearance, for not only did her parents squander time and money in a non-ending attempt to locate her, but Uncle Christopher made many trips to Philadelphia to unravel the mystery, but to no avail. So much for the "Franey Legend."

Uncle Christopher had one practice which displeased my Grandmother, but interested me greatly. On his regular trips to the freight yards, he would frequently return with some unfortunate tramp, or hobo, as they were called in those days, and he would allow his friend to sleep on a cot in our cellar near the furnace. He stoutly maintained that these people would likely freeze to death were they exposed to the fierce winters prevalent at the time. The only condition required of his guest was that he refrain from smoking, once inside the cellar. Uncle Christopher defended his position to my Grandmother stating that there had been times in his life when he had been befriended under similar circumstances.

Every now and then I would meet these strangers in the cellar and for the most part they were eternally grateful for the hospitality. They came from all sections of the country and told of how they travelled and lived under the most trying circumstances.

As the years went by, Uncle Christopher became less active and our happy get togethers in the library became less frequent, which saddened me greatly. He stayed in his room more than ever and I think he knew that his time was coming.

On the night of June 21, 1933, I was to graduate from high school and when he told the family that he felt too tired to attend, I knew the situation was serious, for I had never heard him say that he was tired before. Apologizing for his early retirement, he said good night and went to his room.

He died in his sleep that night, and as far as I am concerned, with him died an era in American Romanticism that will never be seen again.